Spirit and Life

A Franciscan Guide for Spiritual Reflection

Daniel P. Horan, OFM
and
Julianne E. Wallace

KOINONIA PRESS
An Imprint of DatingGod.org Productions

Published by Koinonia Press
An Imprint of DatingGod.org Productions

First Printing October 2013
          Koinonia Press
          Boston, MA
          USA
Cover Image: Scott Sharick/iStockPhoto
Cover Design: Koinonia Press Design Department

ISBN: 0615781167
ISBN-13: 978-0615781160

Horan, Daniel P. (1983 –); Wallace, Julianne E. (1979 –)
     Spirit and Life: A Franciscan Guide for Spiritual Reflection / Daniel P. Horan, OFM and Julianne E. Wallace.

               p.   cm.
          1. Spirituality. 2. Franciscan. 3. Prayer. 4. Education.
I. Title

12 11 10 9 8 7 6 5 4 3 2 1

Poverty is an act of love and liberation. It has redemptive value. If the ultimate cause of human exploitation and alienation is selfishness, the deepest reason for voluntary poverty is love of neighbor. Christian poverty has meaning only as a commitment of solidarity with the poor, with those who suffer misery and injustice.

Gustavo Gutiérrez

Look at the humility of God, and pour out your hearts before Him! Humble yourselves that you may be exalted by Him! Hold back nothing of yourselves for yourselves, that He who gives Himself totally to you may receive you totally!

St. Francis of Assisi

Contents

∾

Acknowledgements

∾

There are many to whom thanks is owed. First among them are Br. Brian Belanger, OFM, whose recognition of the need for a resource such as this on college campuses led to the earliest occasion to develop this program, and Dr. Shannon O'Neill, who was the co-facilitator of this program's initial trial in the Domincan Republic.

Thanks go to Jessica Coblentz and Sr. Margaret Klotz, OSF, both of whom read early versions of this book and offered helpful questions and feedback.

We are grateful to our colleagues in ministry and academia at St. Bonaventure University, Siena College, the Washington Theological Union, and Boston College, who offer a support and inspiring ministry and academic environments.

Finally, we are especially thankful for the gifts and challenges that our students bring to our lives and work. We have both been blessed by the opportunity to serve, educate, and mentor many talented, caring, intelligent, and spiritually inspired students.

Julianne wishes to express particular gratitude to the students of Buffalo State College Newman Center, who were so positively affected by this reflection program and the Francsican tradition during a trip to the St. Francis Inn in Philadelphia with her and who so signficantly shaped her own experience and future experiences as a campus minister.

This book is for our students and for all students wherever they may be on their journey of faith.

Introduction

∾

The journey was long and the group was tired. Having traveled from the upstate New York college campus to a metropolitan airport nearly three hours away to catch a direct flight to the Dominican Republic early in the morning and having spent the better part of that day traveling to their destination, the dozen juniors and seniors that had organized and prepared for a week of academic community engagement in an impoverished community on the outskirts of Santo Domingo were exhausted and ready for bed.

Some of the students had been to this community before; others had never left the continental United States and were witnessing a world unlike anything they had seen before. For a young woman or man around twenty-years-old, seeing how many in the Global South lived for the first time can be a viscerally overwhelming experience. Glances out of the bus window that shuttled the group from the airport to the slums offered unmitigated images of the shift from a landscape of urban life toward a place of forgotten people, toward the world of the poorest in a land where everybody was already poor enough.

Silence was the most noticeable quality of that ride. Whereas the anxious and excited students were chattering and laughing from before sunrise until landing in the eastern nation of Hispaniola, now they were shocked into reverent and reflexive silence. The world is indeed much bigger than their typical middle-class, suburban experience of college in the United States would suggest.

1

And what part do they play in it? Why did even the least financially advantaged among them have so much more than the wealthiest person they encountered outside Santo Domingo? Why is there so much poverty, squalor, and suffering here? Where is God in all of this?

That first night, after settling into the guesthouse of the Franciscan Sisters that run the school for which they were there to work, the thought crossed the minds of the two faculty supervisors – the director of the campus women's center and a Franciscan friar – that perhaps everyone should just call it an early night and go to bed. It had been, after all, a very long day. But wisdom prevailed and the quiet yet persistent voice of the Holy Spirit inspired the group to go ahead with the original plan, to begin the intentional practice of prayer and reflection each evening.

Prayer, scripture, the Franciscan tradition, silence, sharing – all of this led to a powerful experience of the Divine in the world, offered a sense of communal understanding, and provided a structure for deep reflection and meaningful processing that continued throughout the trip.

This was an experiment and the result of the experiment led to this book.

The Origin and Need for This Reflection Guide
This reflection guide was initially born out of necessity. Over the last few years it has become increasingly commonplace for colleges and universities to integrate some sort of immersion or service-learning experience into undergraduate curricula and extra-curricular activities sponsored by campus-ministry offices, student associations, and academic departments. While most schools are very good about planning and actualizing such trips and activities, it became clear that few schools offered

their faculty, staff, and students a guide for reflection and processing the often-times intense experiences of their journeys of action and solidarity. Furthermore, even if there were impromptu times and spaces for "debriefing" or "processing," these moments of sincere and emotional sharing might not take place within the context of prayer or faith sharing.

In the fall semester of 2010 Fr. Daniel Horan, OFM, who was teaching in the department of religious studies at Siena College, was approached by Br. Brian Belanger, OFM, who served as the director of the very active international studies program there, and asked if he could develop a theologically sound and expressly *Franciscan* program for spiritual reflection for trips like the one Fr. Dan was set to help co-lead to the Dominican Republic with Dr. Shannon O'Neill. The idea was that rather than rely on possible impromptu reflection sessions during these immersion and service trips, there could be a standard resource that was reliable, simple to follow, easily adaptable, and flexible enough to accommodate a variety of different experiences. The test run of the earliest structure was the immersion and service trip in the spring of 2011 to the Dominican Republic, but it was envisioned that a program of this sort could be developed for adoption in domestic trips, daylong and other shorter service opportunities, classroom use and ongoing spiritual reflection on academic community engagement.

The need for a reflection guide such as this was not limited to Siena College, a Franciscan school near Albany, NY. Soon after the initial run of the program in the Dominican Republic, word spread among campus ministry colleagues and soon requests came to Fr. Dan for access to the draft guide. One of the first to adopt the draft version of *Spirit and Life* for use in domestic service experiences was Julianne Wallace, who at that time was a campus minister at Buffalo State College. She used the program with her students at an inner-city soup kitchen in Philadelphia and found it helpful. She continued to use it when she became a campus minister at St. Bonaventure University, one of the oldest Franciscan universities in North America, where she currently works. Julianne's frequent use and adaptation of the reflection guide gave her insight into little details that could be tweaked or expanded to accommodate better the sorts of experiences that arose during her programs. Her background in liturgy and sacramental theology also proved a valuable resource in developing the prayers of this book.

In a surprisingly short amount of time word about *Spirit and Life* began to spread from campus ministers like Julianne and her colleagues to pastors and on-site program directors of direct-service ministries. Requests came in from organizers at urban ministry sites and from parish leaders who were taking parishioners on service trips to have access to *Spirit and Life* in its earliest iteration. The enduring appeal of the program, its sound theological grounding, its ease of facilitation and use, and its remarkable adaptability suggested that a more-accessible format of a fully developed program was needed.

Fr. Dan enlisted the assistance of Julianne to work on developing a fuller edition of the program. What follows in this book is the result of their collaboration, the theological vision, Franciscan scholarship, and program structure and format of Fr. Dan's original project matched with the practical wisdom and pragmatic campus-ministry experience of Julianne in the field and on the road with students. In addition to her experience as a campus minister and director of liturgy for the world-renowned Franciscan Institute, Julianne served as a Franciscan Volunteer Minister in Wilmington, DE for a year after earning her Master of Theological Studies degree and before entering campus ministry work full time. The experience of an extended direct-service ministry also gave her a unique perspective on how to faciliate faith formation and spiritual reflection for those engaging in this sort of service or cultural immersion.

The Vision of *Spirit and Life*

The final project that is presented here is designed for use by both the facilitators (faculty, staff, parish leaders, campus ministers, and so on) and all other members of the group. Rather than develop something akin to a "facilitator's guide" and a "participant book," it was acknowledged that experiences of service and cultural immersion affect, shape, and challenge all who participate. Therefore, all the material, resources, and instructions one would need to lead the group in prayer and reflection during a service trip, immersion experience, or academic community engagement activity can be found in this book. Some of the material, for example the appendix at the back of the book, might not be of particular interest or value to all members of the group. However, such material offers further resources and the appendix, in particular, provides the theological and historical grounding and vision for this entire guide.

The size, content, and layout of the book were designed to make it as user friendly as possible. Its relative inexpensiveness was planned to make the book as accessible to all as possible in order to encourage each member of the group to have his or her own copy. Space is provided throughout the book for notes and reflections, which makes this book something of a personal journal too. Participants should feel comfortable marking up, underlining, annotating readings, and jotting thoughts, prayers, and reflections throughout. Just as each member of such a group carries their memories and experiences forward with them, so too this guide may become a resource of scripture, prayer, readings, and reflections to take into the future and return to from time to time.

There is no "right" or "wrong" way to use this guide. How it is adapted and used should be decided by the facilitators and group members according to the context of their particular experience. The purpose of the guide is to provide a structure and a collection of resources, the individual parts of which will be explained further in the next section. There are, in total, six days in addition to a closing day with the familiar structure of the program. For experiences that are shorter, the leader of prayer and reflection might select from among the different days – they need not be followed in sequential order. For experiences that are longer, the leader of prayer and reflection might return to previously used days or create his or her own daily program following the general structure of the guide.

The ultimate vision of this guide is to provide the most helpful context for spiritual reflection on the experiences of the group, following the spiritual and theological heritage of the Franciscan tradition. Groups do not have to be from a Franciscan school, parish, or ministry site to use this resource – the wisdom and tradition of St. Francis and St. Clare of Assisi speak to the hearts of women and men in all places and times.

Structure of the Program

☙

PART I. PRE-PROGRAM PRAYER/REFLECTION

Some days or weeks prior to the scheduled departure date, in conjunction with the regularly scheduled planning session of the group, a time would be set aside for the facilitator of the program to invite the participants to pray and reflect on scripture and material from the Franciscan tradition. Following a *Lectio Divina* format, which is a slow and deliberate reading of and reflection on the Scriptures, the participants would be encouraged to share their reflections on the readings/sources, while also sharing their hopes, fears, expectations for the experience in light of the readings/sources.

PART II. PRE-PROGRAM MISSION SERVICE

Ideally, this mission service would take place within a liturgical context, preferably after Communion during the campus's weekly Sunday Celebration of the Eucharist immediately preceding the group's departure. The principal celebrant (or another minister, campus minister, etc.) would, after the 'Prayer after Communion,' invite those going on a service trip or immersion experience to come forward at which point the entire campus ecclesial community would be invited to pray with and for the participants.

PART III. DAYS ONE THROUGH SIX

- Prayer Service
- Scripture, Franciscan, Scriptural Readings,
- Reflection
- Sharing

PART IV. CLOSING DAY

The closing day features a prayer service and reflection session that resembles the previous three days' programs. The structure of the closing day is designed to be integrative and deliberately engage the liminality of crossing the physical and metaphoric borders of the experience to return to campus.

PART V. POST-PROGRAM PRAYER/REFLECTION

Some days or weeks after the experience – with enough time intervening to allow for individual processing of the experience, but not too much time so the experience is still fresh in the memories of the participants and relevant – the facilitator will lead the group in a program of prayer and reflection that offers a post-programmatic "spiritual debriefing" of what took place, both in a temporal sense and spiritual/emotional/psychological sense. Emphasis will be placed, drawing on Scripture and the sources, on the continuing relevance of the service or immersion experience for the lives of the participants.

> How have you been changed?
> Where do we go from here?
> What else is there to do?
> How has my faith, prayer, relationship with God

been affected by this experience? And so on.

How to use this Reflection Guide

Each of the following prayers services is designed to be flexible and allow for adaptability with your specific service group. The structure for each evening is as follows:

I.   CALL TO PRAYER
II. OPENING PRAYER
III. SCRIPTURE READING
IV. FRANCISCAN READING
V.   GROUP REFLECTION
VI. CLOSING PRAYER

Taking into account this structure, here are some things to keep in mind for each participant in the reflection as you plan and implement each time and celebration of prayer.

Leading Prayer (The Prayer and Reflection Leader)

The prayer and reflection leader can be any person in the group (and the leader or leaders can differ each evening). The prayer and refelction leader sets the pace and tone for each evening of prayer. Leaders are responsible for appointing or soliciting readers for the particular service, leading the group reflection each time, and making any other adaptations or modifications to the prayer service (see below for ideas on how to modify each service).

The prayer and reflection leader should also be attentive to the silence of prayer. The prayer and reflection leader should leave a good amount of time for silence so that participants may reflect on the proclaimed Word, the reflections shared by participants, while maintaining a spirit of prayer, calm, and centeredness throughout.

Proclamation of The Word (The Lector)

The prayer and reflection leader appoints or solicits one or two lectors for each service. The lector should make sure to take his or her time and proclaim the readings SLOWLY and CLEARLY. The lector should let every word resound through the room so that each member of the group can hear, understand, and reflect on the reading at a comfortable and unrushed pace. In order to be confident and comfortable, it is suggested that the appointed or volunteer lector read his or her particular reading out loud one or two times in private for practice before proclaiming the Word in the group.

Modifications To The Service

These prayer services are flexible enough to be modified. Participants should feel comfortable using this reflection guide to help direct, inspire, and assist in creating a meaningful space and structure for prayer and reflection. Music can be added as a reflective or participative feature. There is also room to substitute the suggested prayers with poems, or reflections that participants have created during their time on or in advance of the service trip. It is up to the leader of prayer for each particular service to determine how each reflection will ultimately take shape according to the spirit of the group.

Pre-Program Prayer & Reflection

∾

The group facilitator or some delegated person, perhaps a student leader, should serve as the prayer and reflection leader for the pre-program prayer and reflection. Some weeks or days prior to the group's departure, the group should gather and join in an opportunity to pray and reflect on the expectations, anxieties, hopes and fears of the group participants, while seeking to be open to the guidance of the Holy Spirit while away from campus on this immersion or service experience.

I. INVITATION TO PRAYER
The prayer and reflection leader can use this or a similar invitation:

Let us take a moment of silence to enter into a spirit of prayer and reflection...

II. OPENING PRAYER
The prayer and reflection leader may use this or a similar opening prayer:

Most High, Good God,
As we gather together in your spirit of love and solidarity,
may we be open to your inspiration
and attentive to your Word.
We are called to be instruments of God's peace in the world,
strengthen us with a sense of your justice and guide us with
a sense of your compassion.

11

We reflect on our hopes and joys,
anxieties and fears
about our trip and experience.
Help us to see that you are present with us now and always,
open our eyes to where our presence will meet the needs of
the world.
We pray to become Holy Fools like St. Francis of Assisi,
that we may not be inhibited in doing your work because
of our own insecurities or fears.
We ask all these things in your Holy Name.
AMEN.

III. READING FROM SCRIPTURE

After the opening prayer, the prayer and reflection leader invites the person who will read the Scripture passage to read it aloud (or the leader may do it), careful to read it SLOWLY and CLEARLY.

A Reading from
The Gospel According to Luke

Jesus said to them, "The harvest is abundant but the laborers are few; so ask the master of the harvest to send out laborers for his harvest. Go on your way...Carry no moneybag, no sack, no sandals; and greet no one along the way.

Into whatever house you enter, first say, 'peace to this household.' If a peaceful person lives there, your peace will rest on him; but if not, it will return to you. Stay in the same house and eat and drink what is offered to you, for the laborer deserves his payment. Do not move about from one house to another.

Whatever town you enter and they welcome you, eat what is set before you, cure the sick in it and say to them, 'The kingdom of God is at hand for you.' Whatever town you enter and they do not receive you, go out into the streets and say, 'the dust of your town that clings to our feet, even that we shake off against you.'

Yet know this: the Kingdom of God is at hand."

After the reading from Scripture, the prayer and reflection leader will invite the group to pause for a short time to reflect on the reading.

IV. READING FROM THE FRANCISCAN SOURCES

The prayer and reflection leader, after an adequate time for quiet, private reflection on the Scripture reading, will invite the person who will read the Franciscan text to read the following or a similar passage, careful to read it SLOWLY and CLEARLY.

A selection from *The Life of St. Francis*
By Thomas of Celano

Meanwhile, the holy man of God, having changed his habit and rebuilt that church, moved to another place near the city of Assisi, where he began to rebuild a certain church that had fallen into ruin and was almost destroyed. After a good beginning he did not stop until he had brought all to completion.

One day the Gospel was being read in that church about how the Lord sent out his disciples to preach. The holy man of God, who was attending there, in order to understand better the words of the Gospel, humbly begged the priest after celebrating the solemnities of the Mass to explain the Gospel to him.

The priest explained it all to him thoroughly line by line. When he heard that Christ's disciples should not possess gold or silver or money, or carry on their journey a wallet or a sack, not bread nor a staff, nor to have shoes nor two tunics, but they should preach the kingdom of God and penance, the holy man, Francis, immediately exulted in the spirit of God.

"This is what I want," he said, "this is what I seek, this is what I desire with all my heart." The holy father [St. Francis], overflowing with joy, hastened to implement the words of salvation, and did not delay before he devoutly began to put into effect what he had heard.

Immediately he took off the shoes from his feet, put down the staff from his hands, and, satisfied with one tunic, exchanged his leather belt for a cord. After this, he made for himself a tunic showing the image of the cross.

He made it poor and plain, a thing that the world would never covet. As for the other things he heard, he set about doing them with great care and reverence. For he was no deaf hearer of the Gospel; rather, he committed everything he heard to his excellent memory and was careful to carry it out to the letter.

The prayer leader can now invite the group to again pause for a few moments of silent reflection on the reading.

V. GROUP REFLECTION AND SHARING
The prayer leader now invites the group to share some reflection time with one another about their expectations, fears, anxieties, joys and hopes for the forthcoming trip. Special attention should be given to re-

lecting on these feelings and expectations in light of the readings from Scripture and the Franciscan sources.

The prayer leader may opt to go first, in order to help the other members of the group feel more comfortable sharing. Some reflection questions posed to the group might include, but are not limited to:

- **What are you most excited about for this experience? What fears do you have?**
- **How do you understand Jesus's instruction to the disciples? In what way does this passage speak to you and your experience?**
- **St. Francis was very inspired by this reading from the Gospel. In what ways might his following the Gospel inspire us as a group?**

VI. CLOSING PRAYER

After the group has had plenty of time to share and reflect, the prayer leader invites the group to conclude the prayer and reflection with this prayer or something similar.

Let Us Pray...

Good and Gracious God,
As we prepare to leave on this journey,
Help us be like St. Francis and your own disciples,
In all that we do and wherever we go,
let us be proclaimers of the Kingdom of God.
Give us the strength not to be discouraged when
we are met with adversity and challenge.
Provide us with an abundance of love, courage and
joy, so that we may be the face of Christ

to all we encounter.
May we be driven by our deepest desire to bring
your peace and your love to those who long for you
the most.
We ask this through Christ our Lord,
AMEN.

∾

Notes & Reflections

_____

_____

_____

_____

_____

_____

_____

_____

_____

_____

_____

_____

_____

_____

Pre-Program Mission Service

∾

At a time of the facilitator and campus chaplain's choosing, the group will be invited to participate in one of the campus's regularly scheduled community liturgies. During this liturgy, the group will be called forward to receive the presider's blessing and the community's affirmation of prayer and support for the forthcoming journey. This could take place after the Prayers of the Faithful and before the preparation of the altar or after the Prayer after Communion and before the final blessing.

I. INVITATION TO PRAYER

The presider welcomes the group to come forward in this or some similar fashion:

On behalf of the gathered community of _____, I invite those who will be traveling to _____ to come forward.

The presider, after those members of the group have come forward, continues:

As Jesus sent his disciples into the world to preach the Gospel and announce the Kingdom of God;

And as St. Francis of Assisi, hearing that instruction from the LORD, likewise answered the call to journey into the world, serving others in solidarity;

We, the campus (or parish, etc.) community of
_____, recognize your own embrace of the
LORD's invitation to follow Him in humble service.

Know that while you are traveling and living among
those whom you have been called to serve we will be joined
with you in a spirit of prayer and loving support.

The presider now invites the congregation to join in offering a prayer of blessing for the group.

Let Us Pray...

Most High, Glorious God,
in every age you have chosen servants
to proclaim your Word to the ends of the earth,
witnessing the Gospel in word and deed.
Hear our prayer for our sister(s) and brother(s)
assembled before us.
Fill them with your Spirit that they might
have the mind that was in Jesus Christ,
that openness and humility modeled by St. Francis, and a
willingness to do your will at all times.
We ask this in your Name,
AMEN.

Day One

Following the basic model initiated during the pre-program prayer and reflection session, the group will engage in a similar structure of prayer and reflection guided by passages from Scripture and selections from the Franciscan sources.

I. INVITATION TO PRAYER

The prayer and reflection leader can use this or a similar invitation:

Let us take a moment of silence to enter into a spirit of prayer and reflection...

II. OPENING PRAYER

The prayer and reflection leader can use this or a similar opening prayer:

My Lord God,
I have no idea where I am going.
I do not see the road ahead of me.
I cannot know for certain where it will end.
Nor do I really know myself,
and the fact that I think that I am following your will does
not mean that I am actually doing so.
But I believe that the desire to please you does in fact please
you.

And I hope I have that desire in all that I am doing.
I hope that I will never do anything apart from that desire.
And I know that if I do this you will lead me by the right road though I may know nothing about it.
Therefore I will trust you always though I may seem to be lost and in the shadow of death.
I will not fear,
for you are ever with me, and you will never leave me to face my perils alone.
AMEN.

By Thomas Merton, OCSO,
from *Thoughts In Solitude*

III. READING FROM SCRIPTURE

After the opening prayer, the prayer and reflection leader invites the person who will read the Scripture passage to read it aloud (or the leader may do it), careful to read it SLOWLY and CLEARLY.

A Reading from
The Gospel According to Luke

Then Jesus said to all, "If anyone wishes to come after me, he must deny himself and take up his cross daily and follow me. For whoever wishes to save his life will lose it, but whoever loses his life for my sake will save it.
What profit is there for one to gain the whole world yet lose or forfeit himself [or herself]?

IV. READING FROM THE FRANCISCAN SOURCES

The prayer and reflection leader, after an adequate time for quiet, private reflection on the Scripture reading, will invite the person who will read he Franciscan text to read the following or a similar passage, careful to read it SLOWLY and CLEARLY.

A Selection from *The Major Life of St. Francis*
by St. Bonaventure

From that time on, as [Francis] was removing himself from the pressure of public business, he would eagerly beg the divine kindness to show him what he should do. When the flame of a heavenly desire intensified in him by the practice of frequent prayer, and already, out of his love for a heavenly home, he despised all earthly things as nothing; he realized that he had found a hidden treasure, and, like a wise merchant, planned to buy the pearl he had found by selling everything.

Nevertheless, how he should do this, he did not yet know; except that it was suggested to his spirit that a spiritual merchant must begin with contempt for the world and a knight of Christ with victory over one's self.

V. GROUP REFLECTION AND SHARING

The prayer and reflection leader now invites the group to share some reflection time with one another about their expectations, fears, anxieties, joys and hopes for the trip. Special attention should be given to reflecting on these feelings and expectations in light of the readings from Scripture and the Franciscan sources.

The prayer and reflection leader may opt to go first, in order to help the other members of the group feel more comfortable sharing. Some reflection questions posed to the group might include, but are not limited to:

- Did you see God today? Can you describe that experience?
- Where and in what ways was God present in what you did today?
- Does God have an opinion on the situation here? How do you know?
- What is the connection between your faith and what you did today?

VI. CLOSING PRAYER

After the group has had plenty of time to share and reflect, the prayer and reflection leader invites the group to conclude the prayer and reflection with this prayer or something similar.

Let Us Pray...

Dear God of all beginnings,
from the beginning of creation your Spirit has
been present among us:
renewing,
reviving,
returning us to you.
Aware of your creative power and presence
we know that all things are possible,
and we are ready to embrace the unknown.
But we tremble,
at times fearful of what might lie ahead on the journey.
We offer our uncertainty,
restlessness,
uneasiness,

and fear;
We offer our enthusiasm,
excitement,
energy,
and hope to you!
Keep us mindful of your presence as we move forward,
grant us the courage and love to do your will.
AMEN.

∽

Notes & Reflections

_____

_____

_____

_____

_____

_____

_____

_____

_____

_____

_____

_____

_____

_____

Day Two

Following the basic model initiated during the pre-program prayer and reflection session, the group will engage in a similar structure of prayer and reflection guided by passages from Scripture and selections from the Franciscan sources.

I. INVITATION TO PRAYER
The prayer and reflection leader can use this or a similar invitation:

Let us take a moment of silence to enter into a spirit of prayer and reflection...

II. OPENING PRAYER
The prayer and reflection leader can use this or a similar opening prayer:

**Good and Gracious God,
As we continue forward on this journey,
Help us to rid ourselves of needless anxiety,
and give us the strength to put on the heart of Francis
as we give of ourselves with joy and exultation.
Let us be motivated by the in breaking of your kingdom
around us, and not be our own fears and insecurities.
Give us the heart to bring your love, compassion and joy
to all we serve,
because it is through this joy that your human family be-**

comes one within the Kingdom of God.
AMEN.

III. READING FROM SCRIPTURE

After the opening prayer, the prayer and reflection leader invites the person who will read the Scripture passage to read it aloud (or the leader may do it), careful to read it SLOWLY and CLEARLY.

A Reading from
The Gospel According to Matthew

"I tell you, do not worry about your life, what you will eat or what you will drink, or about your body, what you will wear. Is not life more than food, and body more than clothing? Therefore do not worry, saying, 'What will we eat?' or 'What will we drink?' or 'What will we wear?' But strive first for the Kingdom of God and God's righteousness, and all these things will be given to you as well."

IV. READING FROM THE FRANCISCAN SOURCES

The prayer and reflection leader, after an adequate time for quiet, private reflection on the Scripture reading, will invite the person who will read the Franciscan text to read the following or a similar passage, careful to read it SLOWLY and CLEARLY.

A Selection from *The Life of St. Francis*
by Thomas of Celano

The Father of the poor, the poor Francis ... moved by a great feeling of pity, in order to help the poor in some way, used to approach the rich people of this world during the coldest times of the year, asking them to loan him their cloaks or furs. As they responded even more gladly than the blessed father asked, he used to say to them, "I shall accept this from you only on the condition that you never expect to have it retuned." The first poor man who happened to meet him, he would then clothe with whatever he had received, exulting and rejoicing.

V. GROUP REFLECTION AND SHARING

The prayer and reflection leader now invites the group to share some reflection time with one another about their expectations, fears, anxieties, joys and hopes for the trip. Special attention should be given to reflecting on these feelings and expectations in light of the readings from Scripture and the Franciscan sources.

The prayer and reflection leader may opt to go first, in order to help the other members of the group feel more comfortable sharing. Some reflection questions posed to the group might include, but are not limited to:

- Where have we seen God today?
- What are the concrete actions that we might be called to do in response to the needs of our world?
- How is God present present in the lives and activities of the group and in the lives of the community we are working in this week?

VI. CLOSING PRAYER

After the group has had plenty of time to share and reflect, the prayer and reflection leader invites the group to conclude the prayer and reflection with this prayer or something similar.

Let Us Pray...

God of Life,
give us a vision of our earthly journey.
Guide us on our pilgrimage through this world.
Be our constant companion as we find our way.
Help us when we get lost.
Strengthen us in times of fear.
Grant us the courage to cross the borders that divide
and break down the walls that exclude.
May we offer a welcome to all,
especially our neighbor in need.
And at the end of our sojourn,
as we cross the border of death,
lead us to our true homeland,
where we hope to know at least your eternal embrace
and be united as one body in Christ.
AMEN.

Prayer by Daniel G. Groody, CSC,
University of Notre Dame

∽

Notes & Reflections

Day Three

∾

Following the basic model initiated during the pre-program prayer and reflection session, the group will engage in a similar structure of prayer and reflection guided by passages from Scripture and selections from the Franciscan sources.

I. INVITATION TO PRAYER

The prayer and reflection leader can use this or a similar invitation:

Let us take a moment of silence to enter into a spirit of prayer and reflection...

II. OPENING PRAYER

The prayer and reflection leader can use this or a similar opening prayer:

**O God,
You gave Francis the grace to be simple with the simple,
humble with the humble,
and poor with the poor.
May we, like him, be brother and sister to all.
We ask this in your name.
AMEN.**

III. READING FROM SCRIPTURE

After the opening prayer, the prayer and reflection leader invites the person who will read the Scripture passage to read it aloud (or the leader may do it), careful to read it SLOWLY and CLEARLY.

A Reading from
The Gospel According to Matthew

"Do not store up for yourselves treasures on Earth, where moth and rust consume and where thieves break in and steal; but store up for yourselves treasures in heaven, where neither moth nor rust consumes and where thieves do not break in and steal. For where your treasure is, there you heart will be also."

IV. READING FROM THE FRANCISCAN SOURCES
The prayer and reflection leader, after an adequate time for quiet, private reflection on the Scripture reading, will invite the person who will read the Franciscan text to read the following or a similar passage, careful to read it SLOWLY and CLEARLY.

A Selection from
The Later Rule of 1223 of St. Francis

Let the brothers [and sisters] not make anything their own, neither house, nor place, nor anything at all. As pilgrims and strangers in the world, serving the Lord in poverty and humility, let them go seeking alms with confidence, and they should not be ashamed because, for our sakes, our Lord made Himself poor in this world. This is that sublime height of most exalted poverty which has made you heirs of the Kingdom of Heaven, poor in temporal things, but exalted in virtue.

V. GROUP REFLECTION AND SHARING

The prayer and reflection leader now invites the group to share some reflection time with one another about their expectations, fears, anxieties, joys and hopes for the trip. Special attention should be given to reflecting on these feelings and expectations in light of the readings from Scripture and the Franciscan Sources.

The prayer and reflection leader may opt to go first, in order to help the other members of the group feel more comfortable sharing. Some reflection questions posed to the group might include, but are not limited to:

• In the Gospel of Matthew, Jesus says "where your treasure is, there your heart will be also." Where is your heart?
• How has this experience led you to examine where you put your energy, time, effort?
• What is the Spirit leading you to see about yourself and about the world?

VI. CLOSING PRAYER

After the group has had plenty of time to share and reflect, the prayer and reflection leader invites the group to conclude the prayer and reflection with this prayer or something similar.

Let Us Pray…

O most High and Loving God,
This week you are calling us to examine our treasures of the world and our treasures of the heart.
Open our minds to understand, as Francis did,
that through human poverty and a simple life,

we attain a joy that cannot be attained by means of any worldly treasure.

Open our hearts to see the simple joy on the faces of all those that we serve,

and allow our lives to be forever changed by the grace and humility of our impoverished brothers and sisters.

We ask this through Christ our Lord,

AMEN.

Notes & Reflections

Day Four

∾

Following the basic model initiated during the pre-program prayer and reflection session, the group will engage in a similar structure of prayer and reflection guided by passages from Scripture and selections from the Franciscan sources.

I. INVITATION TO PRAYER
The prayer and reflection leader can use this or a similar invitation:

Let us take a moment of silence to enter into a spirit of prayer and reflection...

II. OPENING PRAYER
The prayer and reflection leader can use this or a similar opening prayer:

**Most Loving God,
from whom all good comes,
grant us discerning hearts.
Teach us to contemplate your wisdom, power,
and goodness in all who bear your image and likeness.
Guide us to love as you have called us to love
and to live as you have called us to live.
We ask this in your name.
AMEN.**

III. READING FROM SCRIPTURE

After the opening prayer, the prayer and reflection leader invites the person who will read the Scripture passage to read it aloud (or the leader may do it), careful to read it SLOWLY and CLEARLY.

A Reading from
The Book of The Prophet Isaiah

Is this not the fast that I choose: to loose the bonds of injustice, to undo the straps of the yoke, to let the oppressed go free, and to break every burden? Is it not to share your bread with the hungry, and bring the homeless poor into your house; when you see the naked, to cover them, and not to hide yourself from your own kin? Then your light shall break forth like the dawn, and your healing shall spring up quickly.

IV. READING FROM THE FRANCISCAN SOURCES

The prayer and reflection leader, after an adequate time for quiet, private reflection on the Scripture reading, will invite the person who will read the Franciscan text to read the following or a similar passage, careful to read it SLOWLY and CLEARLY.

A Selection from
The Admonitions of St. Francis

Where there is charity and wisdom, there is neither fear nor ignorance. Where there is patience and humility, there is neither anger nor disturbance. Where there is poverty with joy, there is neither greed nor avarice. Where there is rest

and meditation, there is neither anxiety nor restlessness. Where there is fear of the Lord to guard an entrance, there the enemy cannot have a place to enter. Where there is a heart full of mercy and discernment, there is neither excess nor hardness of heart.

V. GROUP REFLECTION AND SHARING

The prayer and reflection leader now invites the group to share some re-flection time with one another about their expectations, fears, anxieties, joys and hopes for the trip. Special attention should be given to reflecting on these feelings and expectations in light of the readings from Scripture and the Franciscan sources.

The prayer and reflection leader may opt to go first, in order to help the other members of the group feel more comfortable sharing. Some reflec-tion questions posed to the group might include, but are not limited to:

• Where have you seen God today?
• In what ways are you being called to change your lifestyle to follow the will of God?
• How is the Spirit inviting you to change the way you see the world?

VI. CLOSING PRAYER

After the group has had plenty of time to share and reflect, the prayer and reflection leader invites the group to conclude the prayer and reflection with this prayer or something similar.

Let Us Pray...

Good and Gracious God,
Let each of us have the strength

to be light for those who live in darkness.
Let us help to break the bonds of injustice
by our examples of humility, patience and love.
Through our service and presence this week,
let our hearts be conformed to your own desires for us.
We ask this through Christ our Lord,
AMEN.

∾

Notes & Reflections

_____

_____

_____

_____

_____

_____

_____

_____

_____

_____

_____

_____

_____

_____

Day Five

∾

Following the basic model initiated during the pre-program prayer and reflection session, the group will engage in a similar structure of prayer and reflection guided by passages from Scripture and selections from the Franciscan sources.

I. INVITATION TO PRAYER
The prayer and reflection leader can use this or a similar invitation:

Let us take a moment of silence to enter into a spirit of prayer and reflection...

II. OPENING PRAYER
The prayer and reflection leader can use this or a similar opening prayer:

God of Compassion,
you call us to lives of prayer and good works
to heal the wounds caused by our sins and selfishness
and to bring light to a world so often in darkness.
Keep us mindful of your grace in times of weakness and
difficulty and bring us to true conversion of mind and heart.
We ask this in your name,
AMEN.

III. READING FROM SCRIPTURE

After the opening prayer, the prayer and reflection leader invites the person who will read the Scripture passage to read it aloud (or the leader may do it), careful to read it SLOWLY and CLEARLY.

A Reading from
The Letter of James

Whenever you face trials of any kind, consider it nothing but joy, because you know that the testing of your faith produces endurance; and let endurance have its full effect, so that you may be mature and complete, lacking in nothing. If any of you is lacking in wisdom, ask God, who gives to all generously and ungrudgingly, and it will be given you.

IV. READING FROM THE FRANCISCAN SOURCES

The prayer and reflection leader, after an adequate time for quiet, private reflection on the Scripture reading, will invite the person who will read the Franciscan text to read the following or a similar passage, careful to read it SLOWLY and CLEARLY.

A Selection from
True and Perfect Joy **of St. Francis**

Brother Leo asked Francis: "What is true joy?"

Francis said: "I return from Perugia and arrive here in the dead of night. It's winter time, muddy, and so cold that icicles have formed on the edges of my habit...I come to the gate and, after I've knocked and called for some time, a brother comes and asks: 'who are you?'

'Brother Francis,' I answer.

we have the power to choose our attitude regardless of the circumstances. → Viktor Frankl

'Go away!' he says. 'This is not a decent hour to be wandering about! You may not come in!' When I insist he replies, 'Go away! You are simple and stupid! Don't come back to us again! There are many of us here like you – we don't need you!' I stand at the door and say: 'For the love of God, take me in tonight!' and he replies: 'I will not! Go to another monastery and ask there!'

I tell you this: If I had patience and did not become upset, true joy, as well as true virtue and the salvation of my soul, would consist in this."

V. GROUP REFLECTION AND SHARING

The prayer and reflection leader now invites the group to share some reflection time with one another about their expectations, fears, anxieties, joys and hopes for the trip. Special attention should be given to reflecting on these feelings and expectations in light of the readings from Scripture and the Franciscan sources.

The prayer and reflection leader may opt to go first, in order to help the other members of the group feel more comfortable sharing. Some reflection questions posed to the group might include, but are not limited to:

- Where have you seen God today?
- Where have you experienced trials and suffering for the sake of doing good works?
- Have you found the grace to have 'patience and not become upset' like St. Francis?
- How do you hear the readings speaking to your experience?

VI. CLOSING PRAYER

After the group has had plenty of time to share and reflect, the prayer and reflection leader invites the group to conclude the prayer and reflection with this prayer or something similar.

Let Us Pray…

Gracious and loving God,
Giver of true and perfect joy,
help us to recognize your face of love in every test and trial
this week.
When we become uncomfortable and irritated,
help us to be patient, and give us the wisdom
to be love, to be hope, and to be joy, for all those we encoun-
ter and serve.
For it is through your great joy and sacrifice that we are able
to be love to this world.
We ask this through Christ our Lord,
AMEN.

∽

Notes & Reflections

_____

_____

_____

_____

_____

_____

_____

_____

Day Six

～

Following the basic model initiated during the pre-program prayer and reflection session, the group will engage in a similar structure of prayer and reflection guided by passages from Scripture and selections from the Franciscan sources.

I. INVITATION TO PRAYER
The prayer and reflection leader can use this or a similar invitation:

Let us take a moment of silence to enter into a spirit of prayer and reflection...

II. OPENING PRAYER
The prayer and reflection leader can use this or a similar opening prayer:

O Loving God,
You have drawn us by your love to life the Gospel life.
May we be faithful followers of God's Spirit and
faithful servants of those who most need us in our every-
day lives.
May we be signs of your grace to all we meet.
We ask this in your name,
AMEN.

III. READING FROM SCRIPTURE

After the opening prayer, the prayer and reflection leader invites the person who will read the Scripture passage to read it aloud (or the leader may do it), careful to read it SLOWLY and CLEARLY.

A Reading from
The First Letter of Peter

Above all, maintain constant love for one another, for love covers a multitude of sins. Be hospitable to one another without complaining. Like good stewards of the manifold grace of God, serve one another with whatever gift each of you has received. Whoever speaks must do so as one speaking the very words of God; Whoever serves must do so with the strength that God supplies, so that God may be glorified in all things through Jesus Christ.

IV. READING FROM THE FRANCISCAN SOURCES

The prayer and reflection leader, after an adequate time for quiet, private reflection on the Scripture reading, will invite the person who will read the Franciscan text to read the following or a similar passage, careful to read it SLOWLY and CLEARLY.

A Selection From
The Form of Life **of St. Clare of Assisi**

I admonish and exhort the sisters in the Lord Jesus Christ to beware of all pride, vainglory, envy, avarice, care and anxiety about this world, detraction and murmuring, dissension and division. Let them be always eager to preserve among themselves the unity of mutual love which is the

43

bond of perfection.

V. GROUP REFLECTION AND SHARING

The prayer and reflection leader now invites the group to share some re-flection time with one another about their expectations, fears, anxieties, joys and hopes for the trip. Special attention should be given to reflecting on these feelings and expectations in light of the readings from Scripture and the Franciscan sources.

The prayer and reflection leader may opt to go first, in order to help the other members of the group feel more comfortable sharing. Some reflection questions posed to the group might include, but are not limited to:

- Where have you seen God today?
- How do you or don't you serve one another with the gifts that God has given you? Are you gifts a source of pride, envy, anxiety and so on?
- In what way is God calling you to use your gifts after this service experience?
- Where do you preserve among yourselves mutual love? Where do you need to work on this?

VI. CLOSING PRAYER

After the group has had plenty of time to share and reflect, the prayer and reflection leader invites the group to conclude the prayer and reflection with this prayer or something similar.

Let Us Pray...

Loving God, you have given us many great gifts,
you have showered us with your love and mercy.
Let us not be weighed down by our anxieties and insecu-

rities.

As this week draws near a close, let us continue to use the gifts you have instilled within us.

Give us the courage to speak with the voice of Christ and to serve with the hands of Christ.

Because it is through this service that we become increasingly unified to our brothers and sisters.

We ask this through Christ our Lord,

AMEN.

∾

Notes & Reflections

_____

_____

_____

_____

_____

_____

_____

_____

_____

_____

_____

_____

_____

Closing Day of Prayer & Reflection

∾

Following the basic model initiated during the pre-program prayer and reflection session, the group will engage in a similar structure of prayer and reflection guided by passages from Scripture and selections from the Franciscan sources.

I. INVITATION TO PRAYER
The prayer and reflection leader can use this or a similar invitation:

Let us take a moment of silence to enter into a spirit of prayer and reflection...

II. OPENING PRAYER
The prayer and reflection leader can use this or a similar opening prayer:

Lord, while we announce peace with our lips,
help us to have it even more within our hearts.
May all be moved to peace, goodwill and mercy
as we offer the gift of peace to others.
As we leave our recent, though temporary home,
may the experience of your mercy, love and peace
that we have received here lead us to bring about
Your justice and peace wherever we go.
We ask this in your name.
AMEN.

III. READING FROM SCRIPTURE

After the opening prayer, the prayer and reflection leader invites the person who will read the Scripture passage to read it aloud (or the leader may do it), careful to read it SLOWLY and CLEARLY.

A Reading from
The Gospel According to Matthew

Jesus took Peter, James, and John his brother, and led them up a high mountain by themselves. And he was transfigured before them; his face shone like the sun and his clothes became white as light. And behold, Moses and Elijah appeared to them, conversing with him.

Then Peter said to Jesus in reply,"Lord, it is good that we are here. If you wish, I will make three tents here, one for you, one for Moses, and one for Elijah."

While he was still speaking, behold, a bright cloud cast a shadow over them, then from the cloud came a voice that said, "This is my beloved Son, with whom I am well pleased; listen to him."

When the disciples heard this, they fell prostrate and were very much afraid.

But Jesus came and touched them, saying, "Rise, and do not be afraid." And when the disciples raised their eyes, they saw no one else but Jesus alone.

As they were coming down from the mountain, Jesus charged them, "Do not tell the vision to anyone until the Son of Man has been raised from the dead."

IV. READING FROM THE FRANCISCAN SOURCES

The prayer and reflection leader, after an adequate time for quiet, private reflection on the Scripture reading, will invite the person who will read the Franciscan text to read the following or a similar passage, careful to read it SLOWLY and CLEARLY.

A Selection from *The Life of St. Francis* by Thomas of Celano

Swift to forgive, slow to grow angry, free in nature, remarkable in memory, subtle in discussing, careful in choices, Francis was simple in everything! Strict with himself, kind with others, he was discerning in everything! Because he was very humble, he showed meekness to all people, and duly adapted himself to the behavior of all. Holy among the holy, among sinners he was like one of them.

V. GROUP REFLECTION AND SHARING

The prayer and reflection leader now invites the group to share some reflection time with one another about their expectations, fears, anxieties, joys and hopes for the trip. Special attention should be given to reflecting on these feelings and expectations in light of the readings from Scripture and the Franciscan sources.

The prayer and reflection lead may opt to go first, in order to help the other members of the group feel more comfortable sharing. Some reflection questions posed to the group might include, but are not limited to:

• Where have you seen God in this experience?
• How does the story of Jesus's transfiguration speak to you?
• In what ways are you transformed by your experience and how are you going to bring that experience down from the

mountain?
• How do you allow the experience of the struggles of your fellow brothers and sisters shape the way you engage with others?
• In which aspects of your life do you need to work on this?

VI. CLOSING PRAYER

After the group has had plenty of time to share and reflect, the prayer and reflection leader invites the group to a conclude the prayer and reflection with this prayer or something similar.

Let Us Pray...

O God,
Look with mercy upon our suffering world
and help us believe in the power of your spirit at work among us.
Help us strive always to imitate the way of simplicity, humility, and poverty and always acknowledge the good you do through us.
May the experiences we have had here
imprint in our hearts and help shape who we are as women and men called to be your disciples.
May the good work you have begun in us here continue
wherever we find ourselves in the future, following always the example of Christ and the model of Francis of Assisi.
We ask this in your name,
AMEN.

∽

Notes & Reflections

Post-Program Prayer & Reflection

∾

This prayer service serves as a "spiritual debriefing" of what took place during the days of service or immersion. Plan this service for several days or about a week after the group returns from the trip so that all are well rested, had time to reflect individually, and are now able to share their personal reflections about their experience.

I. INVITATION TO PRAYER
The prayer and reflection leader can use this or a similar invitation:

Let us take a moment of silence to enter into a spirit of prayer and reflection...

II. OPENING PRAYER
The prayer and reflection leader can use this or a similar opening prayer:

**Good and Gracious God,
As we once again gather together as a group,
we offer you praise for the wonderful memories and experiences we have shared together.
We ask that you be present to us in this moment,
and that we may be attentive to your inspiration calling us
to serve your people, our sisters and brothers in Christ.
We ask this through Christ our Lord,**

AMEN.

III. READING FROM SCRIPTURE

After the opening prayer, the prayer and reflection leader invites the person who will read the Scripture passage to read it aloud (or the leader may do it), careful to read it SLOWLY and CLEARLY.

A Reading from
The Gospel According to Matthew

As he was walking by the Sea of Galilee, he saw two brothers, Simon who is called Peter, and his brother Andrew, casting a new into the sea; they were fishermen. He said to them, "Come after me, and I will make you fishers of men." At once they left their nets and followed him. He walked along from there and saw two other brothers, James, the son of Zebedee and his brother John. They were in a boat, with their father Zebedee, mending the nets. He called them, and immediately they left their boat and their father followed him.

He went around all of Galilee, teaching in their synagogues, proclaiming the gospel of the kingdom, and curing every disease and illness among the people. His fame spread to all Syria, and they brought to him all who were sick with various diseases and racked with pain, those who were possessed, lunatics, and paralytics, and he cured them. And great crowds from Galilee, the Decapolis, Jerusalem, and Judea, and from beyond the Jordan followed him.

IV. READING FROM THE FRANCISCAN SOURCES

The prayer and reflection leader, after an adequate time for quiet, private reflection on the Scripture reading, will invite the person who will read the Franciscan text to read the following or a similar passage, careful to read it SLOWLY and CLEARLY.

A Selection from
The Testament **of St. Francis**

The Lord gave me, Brother Francis, thus to begin doing penance in this way: for when I was in sin, it seemed too bitter for me to see lepers. And the Lord Himself led me among them and I showed mercy to them. And when I left them, what had seemed bitter to me was turned into sweetness of soul and body.

And I worked with my hands, and I still desire to work; and I earnestly desire all brothers to give themselves to honest work. Let those who do not know how to work learn, not from desire to receive wages, but for an example and to avoid idleness.

And whoever observes these things, let him be blessed in heaven with the blessing of the Most High Father, and on earth with the blessing of His Beloved Son with the Most Holy Spirit, the Paraclete, and all the powers of heaven and with all the saints. And, as far as I can, I, little brother Francis, your servant, confirm for you, both within and without, this most Holy blessing.

V. GROUP REFLECTION AND SHARING

The prayer and reflection leader now invites the group to share some re-
flection time with one another about their experiences. Special attention
should be given to reflecting on these feelings and experiences in light of
the readings from Scripture and the Franciscan sources.

The prayer and reflection lead may opt to go first, in order to help the
other members of the group feel more comfortable sharing. Some reflec-
tion questions posed to the group might include, but are not limited to:

• What are some of the most profound memories I have
from this experience?

• How has my faith, prayer, and relationship with God been
affected by this experience?

• Where am I feeling called now in light of this service or
immersion experience?

• What actual or practical things are going to change in how
I live my day-to-day life because of this service experience?

VI. CLOSING PRAYER

After the group has had plenty of time to share and reflect, the prayer and
reflection leader invites the group to a conclude the prayer and reflection
with this prayer or something similar.

Let Us Pray...

Wherever we are,
in every place,
at every hour,
at every time of the day,
every day and continually,
let all of us truly and humbly believe,
hold in our heart and love,

honor, adore, serve,
praise and bless,
glorify and exalt,
magnify and give thanks
to the Most High and Supreme Eternal God
Trinity and Unity
Father, Son and Holy Spirit.
AMEN.

Closing Prayer excerpted from
The Earlier Rule ch. XXIII, v. 11

ᦥ

Notes & Reflections

_____

_____

_____

_____

_____

_____

_____

_____

_____

_____

Appendix I

Prophecy and Solidarity[1]
A Theological Grounding for the Program

❧

The following appendix provides an historical and theological context for the reflection series that appears in the previous pages. The daily format, developing over six days, reflects the threefold process (two days at a time) of moving from "Service" to "Solidarity" in an effort to invite those engaged in community service projects, immersion experiences, or academic community engagement to begin a process of metanoia or conversion toward a lifelong witness of Christian prophetic praxis and reflection.

What is it that we offer our students when we offer them a Franciscan education? Recently the trend has been to respond to that question with an eye toward integration of service-learning based pedagogy with core curricular goals and objectives.[2] This, in itself, is an admirable and import-

---

1. This appendix originally appeared as: Daniel P. Horan, "Profit or Prophet? A Franciscan Challenge to Millennials in Higher Education," *The AFCU Journal* 8 (2011): 59-73.

2. The last several volumes of the AFCU Journal offer perspectives along these lines. For a sampling, see: Kevin Godfrey and Kelly Cockrum, "'What are You Serving Today?' How AFCU Member-Schools are Helping Students Integrate the Franciscan Ideal of Service into Their Personal and Professional Lives – Parts One through Four," *The AFCU Journal* 3 (2006): 81-101, *The AFCU Journal* 4 (2007): 73-86, *The AFCU Journal* 5 (2008): 150-158, and *The AFCU Journal* 7 (2010): 143-157; F. Edward Coughlin, "Serving Generously and Loving Rightly: Insights for a Value-Centered Life from the Franciscan Tradition," *The AFCU Journal* 7 (2010): 28-43; Matthew Sills and Timothy Johnson, "Reconstructing the Gift: Using Franciscan

ant component to a well-rounded undergraduate education and should be supported and encouraged. However,
service learning, as such, is not Franciscan.[3] Many colleges
and universities associated with varying religious congre-
gations or traditions emphasize the importance of service to
the community as a constitutive element of a contemporary
liberal arts education. To suggest that service is a core pillar
of Franciscan education is to posit a false monopoly in the
market of effective undergraduate curricula.[4] The suggestion that service learning is not exclusively Franciscan is not
to undermine the significance of its role in today's integrated educational programs. Rather, the question raised in not-
ing this observation is: What about service-learning as it is
done at explicitly Franciscan schools – member institutions
of the AFCU, for example – makes it Franciscan? Or, to put
it yet another way, and perhaps more realistically: What can

Thought to Foster Service Learning," *The AFCU Journal* 7 (2010): 65-79; Charles
Coate and Todd Palmer, "Franciscan-Based Service Learning: The Evolution of a
Service Experience," *The AFCU Journal* 5 (2008): 134-147; and Barbara Spies, "Using Academic Service-Learning to Teach Franciscan Values," *The AFCU Journal* 4
(2007): 66-72.

    3. For an overview of early adaptation and development of so-called
'service-learning' programs at a variety of undergraduate institutions, see Alexan-
der Astin, Linda Sax and Juan Avalos, "Long-Term Effects of Volunteerism During
the Undergraduate Years," *The Review of Higher Education* 22 (1999): 187-202; and,
while specifically geared toward undergraduate education majors, the following
study provides insightful commentary on general community-engagement and
service curricula: Margaret Vickers, Catherine Harris, and Florence McCarthy,
"University-Community Engagement: Exploring Service-Learning Options Within the Practicum," *Asia-Pacific Journal of Teacher Education* 32 (2004): 129-141.

    4. One recent study suggests service as a means for effectively intro-
ducing students to Catholic Social Teaching, thereby transcending charismatic
delimitations in an effort to highlight the more genus-like mission and identity
of all Catholic institutions of higher education. See Jennifer Reed-Bouley, "Social Analysis in Service-Learning: A Way for Students to Discover Catholic Social
Teaching," *Journal of Catholic Higher Education* 27 (2008): 51-64. Likewise, a recent
article in the NCEA journal suggests that what distinguishes service-learning at
so-called secular institutions from that of Catholic ones is precisely the Catholicity
present within the founding tradition of the school. See Kenneth Paulli, "Catholic
Colleges Offer a Purposeful Engagement of the Heard, Heart and Hands with the
Love of Christ," *Momentum* 41 (February/March 2010): 60-63.

be done to make such programs more Franciscan?

Academic community engagement, a phrase I prefer to service-learning, denotes a programmatic effort to introduce students to a new way of conceptualizing the educational experience that moves them beyond the classroom and into local and global communities. In so doing, students are introduced to a new medium of educational content. Whereas educational content is largely associated with text in most liberal arts curricula, the experience of academic community engagement provides students (and instructors) with a new form of learning. As such, academic community engagement becomes a new text, a new lesson plan. In considering community engagement, or service learning, as text, traditionally conceived content-based emphases are de-centered to open a space for creative learning and holistic experiences of education.

I believe that academic community engagement provides a unique opportunity for Franciscan colleges and universities to integrate the explicitly Franciscan dimensions of the various institutions' founding charism into the educational experience of their undergraduates. By refocusing the curriculum to more comprehensively shape academic community engagement to exhibit the values inherent in the Franciscan intellectual and spiritual tradition, AFCU institutions might better distinguish their programs as "Franciscan." This can be done in a number of ways, but I will offer two suggestions for consideration. The first is the challenge of changing the pedagogical grammar of academic community engagement from conceptions resembling civic responsibility, charity, service, and so on, to a more exclusive notion of solidarity. As it will be presented below, solidarity provides the framework for reconsidering one's stance in the world. The intentional self-subordination exhibited in the life and rules (*regulae*) of Francis of Assisi provides a model for an authentically Christian posture or vita evangelica. While institutions representing religious traditions of all sorts and even secular or state universities can provide programs and curricula aimed at instilling civic responsibility, philanthropic interest and community building values in today's young adults, the Franciscan approach to academic community engagement should be less generic in its charge, moving more toward modeling and encouraging lives of Christian discipleship after the examples of Francis and Clare of Assisi.

The second suggestion flows from this first consideration of solidarity as a constitutive element of the Franciscan tradition. Namely, one challenge that the Franciscan tradition should pose to Millennials in higher education is whether these students want to appropriate the increasingly common social norms that support ungoverned desire for social mobility and the accumulation of wealth or do they want to stand apart from such materialistic teleology, instead working toward an ever more integrated sense of prophetic call to live as Christian disciples according to the Franciscan tradition. The meaning of prophecy can vary largely from one authority to the next; therefore, it seems fitting to look within the Franciscan tradition for guidance in explicating its meaning. St. Bonaventure provides us with a helpful theology of prophecy in his *Legenda Major*, in which he draws on the life of Francis to serve as the hagiographical context from within which Bonaventure presents his understanding.

These two suggestions, the emphasis on solidarity in shaping academic community engagement opportunities and the promotion of graduates of Franciscan institutions of higher education as prophets according to the theology of Bonaventure, draw on the call to reach into the rich tradition latent in the very establishment of the AFCU-member colleges and universities.[5] To direct academic community

---

5. For a good overview of this task, see Margaret Carney, "The 'DNA' of

engagement in a manner that seeks to form prophetic graduates whose stance in the world is one of solidarity is not extrinsic to the founding charism, but instead flows from the Franciscan tradition.

This appendix is organized into four sections. The first section is a presentation of the Millennial generation and its propensity toward community service, global connectivity and volunteerism. The second section focuses on the Franciscan call to live in solidarity with the poor, marginalized and all of creation. The third section explores the theology of prophecy in Bonaventure's *Legenda Major* as a source for undergraduate character formation. Finally, the last section offers a recapitulative summary and conclusion that points us onward toward the next step in shaping an explicitly Franciscan form of academic community engagement.

The Millennial Generation and Service

Service is not a foreign concept to members of the Millennial generation, those women and men born in or after 1982.[6] In a recently published popular book titled Generation We, Eric Greenberg and Karl Weber highlight this trend as a significant feature of Millennial affectivity.[7] The authors explain their choice in book title: "They [the Millennials] are also a caring generation, one that appears ready to put the greater good ahead of individual rewards. Hence our preferred name for them – Generation We."[8] Perhaps the primary expression of this generation's "caring" pro-

Franciscan Institutions," *The AFCU Journal* 2 (2005): 1-17.

6. There is some debate about the most appropriate starting year. For our purpose, Millennials are understood as those born in or after 1980 up and through the year 2002. For more see Neil Howe and William Strauss, *Millennials Rising: The Next Great Generation* (New York: Vintage Books, 2000).

7. Eric Greenberg and Karl Weber, *Generation We: How Millennial Youth Are Taking Over America and Changing Our World Forever* (Emeryville, CA: Pachatusan Publishers, 2008).

8. Greenberg and Weber, *Generation We*, 13.

clivity is the service they have elected to engage in from an early age. Greenberg and Weber explain:

> Volunteerism is unusually high among Millennials. According to UCLA's American Freshman survey – conducted for the past 40 years with several hundred thousand respondents each year – 83 percent of entering freshman in 2005 volunteered at least occasionally during their high school senior year, the highest ever measured in this survey. Seventy-one percent said they volunteered on a weekly basis. (Some data sources indicate that rates of volunteering among Millennials may actually have been highest right after – and presumably in reaction to – 9/11, but difference in question wording and population surveyed prevent definitive judgment on this possibility). Generation We is deeply concerned about the common good. They also believe in social change – and they are ready, even eager, to play their role in making positive changes happen.[9]

While Greenberg and Weber seek to identify general characteristics from within the Millennial cohort, additional studies suggest that the affective religiosity of today's young adults also reflects an increase in service as a priority or second-nature dimension of the collective generational personality. In other words, not only are Millennials across class, race, ethnicity and geographic location being identified as more likely to engage in direct service or some form of volunteerism than previous generations, but such action has also been linked to this generation's religious self-perception.

The authors of the recent book American Catholics Today note that, while young adults attach some importance

---

9. Greenberg and Weber, *Generation We*, 31-32.

to their identity as Catholics, Millennials do so to a lesser degree than previous generations.[10] Additionally, Christian Smith and Melinda Denton, in their 2005 study on the religiosity and spirituality of American teenagers, maintain that among U.S. Christian teenagers, Catholics consistently scored lower on most measures of religiosity.[11] It would seem that such statistics yield a portrait of the Millennial generation that is not open to religious expression, participation or corporate membership, but such an interpretation is only possible when relying upon a metric that measured previous generations' affective religiosity. Renowned sociologist Robert Wuthnow supports this claim for a broader perspective of Millennial religiosity, suggesting, "Young adults overwhelmingly opt for personal experience over church doctrines."[12] He goes on to assert that an appropriate way to view Millennial spirituality is not through the adherence to a particular set of doctrinal canons, a simple test of religiosity for previous generations, but to understand that today's young adults are "spiritual tinkerers" or "spiritual bricoleurs."[13] By this categorization, Wuthnow is not suggesting that Millennials are necessarily adopting a spirituality of syncretism. Rather, this generation makes choices about which aspects of their religious tradition's normative

---

10. William D'Antonio, James Davidson, Dean Hoge and Mary Gautier, *American Catholics Today: New Realities of Their Faith and Their Church* (Lanham, MD: Rowman & Littlefield Publishing, 2007), 34-35. For more on the religious identity of Millennial Catholics see Thomas Rausch, *Being Catholic in a Culture of Choice* (Collegeville, MN: The Liturgical Press, 2006), esp. 1-19; and Dean Hoge, "Religious Commitments of Young Adult Catholics," in *Inculturation and the Church in North America*, ed. T. Frank Kennedy (New York: Herder and Herder, 2006), 198-214.

11. Christian Smith and Melinda Lundquist Denton, *Soul Searching: The Religious and Spiritual Lives of American Teenagers* (New York: Oxford University Press, 2005), 194.

12. Robert Wuthnow, *After the Baby Boomers: How Twenty- and Thirty-Somethings are Shaping the Future of American Religion* (Princeton: Princeton University Press, 2007), 133.

13. Wuthnow, *After the Baby Boomers*, 134-135.

Catholic religious expression

expressions they wish to embrace, while also appropriating other, and often new, expressions of faith.

Whereas previous generations identified Catholic Christianity with factors such as participation in the sacraments and church attendance, today's young adults are more likely to associate religious experience with service, volunteerism and Catholic Social Teaching. Service has emerged as a form of religious expression often gone unstudied by generational observers and sociologists.[14] What we can glean from this trend is that Millennials, while possibly uninterested in the traditional or normative tenets of Catholic religious expression, are in fact appropriating contemporary avenues to the divine and exploring new expressions of Catholic religiosity.[15]

What this means for Franciscan institutions of higher education is that, if this service-oriented generational trend continues, incoming students will already be predisposed to service as a regular feature of everyday life. On one hand, this presents the challenge for administrators and educators at Franciscan colleges and universities to move beyond simply introducing opportunities for academic community engagement. For what had once been a novel feature of an innovative curricular program, is now something that today's young adults might take for granted. On the other hand, this presents a unique opportunity for Franciscan schools to connect with incoming students who may a priori see academic community engagement as a place of

14. For more see, Wendy Murray Zoba, "Youth Has Special Powers," _ChristianityToday_ 45.2 (February 5, 2001): 57; Megan Sweas, "Marked For Life: Former full-time volunteers confess that their experiences change them for good," _U.S. Catholic_ 72.7 (July 2007): 12- 17; D'Antonio, et.al, _American Catholics Today_, 93; and Rausch, _Being Catholic in a Culture of Choice_, 12-13.

15. See Sharon Daloz Parks, _Big Questions, Worthy Dreams: Mentoring Young Adults in Their Search for Meaning, Purpose and Faith_ (San Francisco: Jossey-Bass Publishing, 2000), 25-26; Hoge, "Religious Commitments of Young Adult Catholics," 198-214; and Daniel Horan and Melissa Cidade, "'Major' Changes Toward Philosophy and Theology: Interpreting a Recent Trend For Millennials in Catholic Higher Education," _Journal of Catholic Higher Education_ 30 (2011): 133-150.

spiritual encounter. Previous generations, during the earliest years of service-learning based education models, may have had to be "convinced" of the spiritual and educational nexus that such opportunities create for the students. Today's students, it would seem, are much more amenable to these programs and might even expect them.

Shaping academic community engagement programs to reflect the Franciscan tradition requires deliberate attention to students' social, cultural, ecclesiastical and religious locations. In light of the predisposition of Millennials toward service and, in turn, identifying a spiritual or religious dimension in such action, Franciscan institutions of higher education are in a good place to begin offering their students a Franciscan education founded on the eight-hundred-year-old tradition handed down to us by Francis and Clare of Assisi. The first area in need of examination and reconsideration is the language and goal of service. A shift from this sort of discourse toward one that speaks of solidarity better reflects the Franciscan spiritual patrimony of which today's undergraduate students are heirs.

Solidarity: Moving Beyond the Discourse of Service

In an essay on the relationship between Franciscan identity and the university, renowned Franciscan theologian Zachary Hayes introduced the concept of Franciscanism as pertaining to a Christian religious experience. He wrote:

> As a form of Christianity, Franciscanism is first of all a religious movement. The religious dimension is clearly attested to in the life of Francis and in the history of the Order. People have attempted to turn Francis into many things; for example a naïve nature-romantic, a social revolutionary, a rebel against the authority of the Church and such. Whatever may be said of these attempts, they commonly by-

pass what stands out most clearly in Francis's own writings. The deep well-spring of his life from the beginning of his conversion was a religious experience. From this experience he came to perceive God in a distinctive way. He had, likewise, a distinctive perception of Christ. From this starting point he came to his perception of himself and to his vision of humanity and the whole created world. [16]

Hayes identifies religious experience, prior to all other dimensions of Francis's life, as the centerpiece of what makes Franciscanism Franciscan. In light of the Millennial generation's pre-collegiate disposition to engage in service and identify such activity with religious experience, one can see a starting point for dialogue more explicitly related to the Franciscan tradition. A featured component of any form of academic community engagement at a Franciscan institution of higher education should consist in theological reflection shaped, in large part, by the early sources of the Order. Here we might draw on the rich spiritual wisdom in the writings of Francis and Clare, look to the mystical and deeply illustrative theology of Bonaventure, explore the sermons of Anthony of Padua or Bernardine of Siena, or even delve into the ethical and metaphysical work of John Duns Scotus. To do so is to create a space within which contemporary appropriation of the religious experience of those early Franciscan practitioners can be engaged with the religious experiences of those young women and men today.

The intentional and conscious theological – and, therefore, a priori spiritual[17] – reflection on service helps students and facilitators alike transcend the strictures of limited service- or civic-oriented discourse. To reflect on ser-

---

16. Zachary Hayes, "Reflections on a Franciscan University," *Spirit and Life: A Journal of Contemporary Franciscanism* 2 (1992): 98. Italics original.

17. For example, see Ilia Delio, "Is Spirituality the Future of Theology? Insights from Bonaventure," *Spiritus* 8 (Fall 2008): 148-155.

vice within the context of faith and religious experience necessarily opens a wide horizon of encounter with the sacred that elicits ethical challenges to the participants. The status quo of everyday life peppered as it were by direct service becomes subjected to the scrutiny of authentic Gospel living in a way that is not concomitantly present in service-learning or civic engagement as such. Instead, the experience, like that described by Hayes above or found in the early life of Francis himself, becomes the foundation for re-integrating the vita evangelica with the rest of contemporary life. This is what distinguishes Gospel-oriented academic community engagement from other forms of service-learning in higher education. It is the moving beyond the language of service to conceive such experiences as initiatives directed at equipping students with the capacity to reorient their lives from a profit-based, post-collegiate teleology to an explicit stance of solidarity formed in the Franciscan tradition.

In order to unpack this transitional movement toward solidarity as a constitutive component of the Franciscan experience of academic community engagement, we must look at the tradition of evangelical poverty as it relates to the poverty of abjection so often encountered in these experiences of engagement. Gustavo Gutiérrez, largely considered the "Father" of Liberation Theology, explains that poverty within the Christian tradition is generally understood in two ways. There is "material poverty," that is poverty understood in the first sense, and "spiritual poverty," a term that has been both helpful and problematic over the course of Christian history.[18] Material poverty needs little introduction. It is simply the absence of those basic resources that human flourishing requires. Spiritual poverty, a concept that has been used to diminish the demand of certain biblical pericopes on the wealthy and those who minister

---

18. Gustavo Gutiérrez, *A Theology of Liberation*, trans. Caridad Inda and John Eagleson (Maryknoll, NY: Orbis Books, 1988), 162-171.

to the economically comfortable, is rather nuanced and un-clear. Gutiérrez is concerned with exploring a third under-standing of poverty, one that I would suggest aligns itself well with the Franciscan understanding of that evangelical virtue. This third approach is that of intentional poverty as both a form of solidarity and protest. Gutiérrez, drawing on God's own example of kenotic impoverishment through the Incarnation, explains:

> Poverty is an act of love and liberation. It has a re-demptive value. If the ultimate cause of human ex-ploitation and alienation is selfishness, the deepest reason for voluntary poverty is love of neighbor. Christian poverty has meaning only as a commit-ment of solidarity with the poor, with those who suffer misery and injustice. The commitment is to witness to the evil which has resulted from sin and is a breach of communion. It is not a question of ide-alizing poverty, but rather of taking it on as it is – an evil – to protest against it and to struggle to abolish it. As Ricouer says, you cannot really be with the poor unless you are struggling against poverty. Be-cause of this solidarity – which one must manifest itself in specific action, a style of life, a break with one's social class – one can also help the poor and exploited to become aware of their exploitation and seek liberation from it. [19]

As Gutiérrez notes well, solidarity is a comprehensive and integrated stance in the world. Unlike service work or char-ity (as popularly conceived), solidarity requires "specific action, a style of life, a break with one's social class." It is perhaps unreasonable to expect 18-year-olds to so radically adopt a position of solidarity in short order, but it is not

---

19. Gutiérrez, *A Theology of Liberation*, 172.

beyond their capacity to begin to re-imagine what a morally just and particularly Christian life might look like, and then work in ways to make that commitment an ever-more concrete reality. These features of solidarity highlighted by Gutiérrez resound in the life experience of Francis of Assisi.

A young adult himself (born around the year 1182, Francis was about 23- or 24-years-old when he began to change his life), Francis slowly came to live a life of solidarity with the poor and marginalized much in line with the progressive sequence described by Gutiérrez. At first Francis engaged in a concrete, specific action. The Saint's first official biographer, Thomas of Celano, recounts that Francis was at first "changed in mind but not in body" and apparently took his time appropriating the will of God in place of his own, yet he desired to do so even in the earliest stages of his ongoing conversion (1C3:6).[20] It was then through the selling of his father's cloth for money to be used in restoring the church of San Damiano that he began to engage in specific actions. He sought to live at the church, without accumulating wealth associated with income, selling all he could to give to the poor. It was in this transition of lifestyle that Francis exhibited the second characteristic of solidarity Gutiérrez notes. Finally, that famous scene depicting Francis's renouncement of his father and the stability, status and inheritance associated with him, before the bishop marks the definite break with the Saint's social class. No longer was Francis somewhere in the realm of the merchant class and majores of Assisi, but instead intentionally moved to the place of the minores or lesser ones who were often outcast or dismissed.

In essence, whether intentional or not, Francis's movement from a place of power, wealth and security to a social location of vulnerability and minority reflected the

20. Thomas of Celano, *The Life of Saint Francis*, Bk. I, Ch. III, v. 6, in *FAED* 1:187.

self-emptying + solidarity

kenotic character of God becoming human in the Incarnation. It was a self-emptying that made possible the condition for solidarity as opposed to service from another social, economic and cultural place. In solidarity one does not fall prey to the self-gratifying condescension that is rewarded in the "giving" of service to another from a remote location. Instead, solidarity depends on the poverty of Gospel life, modeled by Christ and echoed in Francis, that finds its source in the divestment of one's selfishness and self-centeredness expressed in the disassociation with others. Ilia Delio offers a reflection on this experience of conversion and Gospel living according to the Franciscan tradition when she writes:

> True poverty creates community because it converts self-sufficiency into creative interdependency where the mystery of life unfolds for us. Only those who can see and feel for another can love another without trying to possess the other. Poverty is that free and open space within the human heart that enables us to listen to the other, to respect the other and to trust the other without feeling that something vital will be taken from us...Conversion to poverty and humility is the nucleus of Christian evolution because it is the movement to authentic love; a movement from isolated "oneness" toward mutual relatedness, from individualism toward community, where Christ is revealed in the union of opposites in the web of life. [21]

As Delio notes, the movement toward this poverty lived by Francis and described by Gutiérrez is the constitutive dimension of solidarity called for in authentic Gospel life. To put it another way, Francis, in a reflection on the Eucharist,

---

21. Ilia Delio, "Christian Life in a World of Change," *The AFCU Journal* 7 (2010): 9. Italics original.

expresses the core of this kenotic sense of solidarity that embraces evangelical poverty wholeheartedly. The poverello writes, "Brothers, look at the humility of God, and pour out your hearts before Him! Humble yourselves that you may be exalted by Him! Hold back nothing of yourselves for yourselves, that He who gives Himself totally to you may receive you totally!" (LtOrd 28-29).[22]

To speak of "Franciscan service" is, in some sense, redundant or at least perplexingly obvious. It should go without saying that those steeped in the Franciscan way of living in this world in the form and manner of the Holy Gospel would be present and attentive to the needs of their brothers and sisters in a way reflecting service as it is popularly conceived. However, the action without reflection on the deeper call to conversion as a movement toward solidarity with those being served is to fall short of the Franciscan contribution to Christian living. The challenge of discourse for those shaping programs for students to participate in academic community engagement at Franciscan colleges and universities is to return again to the distinguishing characteristics of Franciscan living that offer poignant contributions to the spiritual formation and social education of today's young adults. There is indeed a *Franciscan* way of education, just as there is a *Franciscan* form of ministry.[23] Instead of instilling a sense of service in our students – a sensibility the Millennial generation is already attuned to as noted above – perhaps we should focus more intentionally on the shaping of that sensibility toward a commitment to Gospel life and ongoing conversion. In doing so, we will certainly encourage students to be better citizens and mem-

22. Francis of Assisi, "A Letter to the Entire Order" vv. 28-29, in *FAED* 1:118.

23. For more on Franciscan ministry, see Daniel Horan, "A Franciscan Approach to Ministry," *Review for Religious* 68 (2009): 132-143; and Michael Blastic, "Contemplation and Compassion: A Franciscan Ministerial Spirituality," *Spirit and Life: A Journal of Contemporary Franciscanism* 7 (1997): 149-177.

bers of society, but we will also highlight the path toward solidarity. Once on the path of conversion toward solidarity with the poor and marginalized of our world, the students will begin to see reality in a new light through the lens of Christian living. What began as a heuristic model of academic community engagement marked by the language of solidarity will hopefully become a hermeneutic of prophetic living.

Franciscan Prophets for Today: Sustaining Solidarity and Christian Living

Unlike many of the other accounts of the life and times of Francis of Assisi, Bonaventure's *Legenda Major* does not follow the typical style and conventions of medieval hagiography. Granted, there are certainly some elements that resonate with the work of hagiographers such as Thomas of Celano and Julian of Speyer, but Bonaventure was more interested in presenting a unique matrix of symbolic theology that posits Francis of Assisi as exemplar, not just of authentic Franciscan living, but as *the* Christian disciple. In his *vita* Bonaventure meticulously fashions a theological framework within which the life of the Saint is situated. There is richness to the style and deeply integrated and interrelated nature of the text, something that has often been overlooked due to the history of particularly unfavorable presuppositions about Bonaventure's governance of the Order as Minister General and misunderstandings about the nature of the *Legenda Major* itself.[24] Despite the absence of critical

---

24. For example, see John Moorman, *The Sources of the Life of Saint Francis* (Manchester: Manchester University Press, 1940); John Moorman, *A History of the Franciscan Order: From its Origins to the Year 1517* (Chicago: Franciscan Herald Press, 1988); Anthony Mockler, *Francis of Assisi: The Wandering Years* (Oxford: Phaedon Press, 1976); and A. G. Little, "Guide to Franciscan Studies," *Études Franciscaines* 40 (1928): 517-533 and 41 (1929): 64-78. There exists perhaps not better example of such a biased perspective on Bonaventure's alleged agenda and participation in 'reshaping' the Franciscan Order, in addition to its unique chronological proximity to Bonaventure's own work, then Angelo Clareno, *A Chronicle or History*

examination of several of the theological themes present in the Legenda Major, the presence of insightful commentary on the meaning of the vita evangelica and Franciscan life more specifically merits consideration. Additionally, what Bonaventure has to offer us by way of a theology of prophecy connects well with the challenge of providing a "Franciscan education" for today's young adults. Whereas the path to conversion exemplified by the movement from the discourse of service to that of solidarity marks the inaugural thrust of Franciscan academic community engagement, the Bonaventurean contribution to theological explication of prophecy provides us with the sustaining reflection on the meaning of Christian discipleship in a Franciscan key. Ultimately, the challenge presented to students at Franciscan colleges and universities should be to live lives driven by profit or exemplified by becoming a prophet. Bonaventure helps us to see how that challenge can be made concrete.

Prophecy is often popularly depicted as the ability to forecast future events. One is a prophet if he or she "saw it coming." And while there is some validity in defining prophecy as such, it is a limited conception of prophecy and one that merits closer examination. Bonaventure's perspective is informed by centuries of antecedent wisdom about and exploration of the subject. In what emerges from both the Hebrew Scriptures and Hellenistic philosophical traditions, the theme of Christian prophecy finds its earliest references in both the canonical and extra-canonical texts of the New Testament era. We read in the New Testament epistolary of the various charisms bestowed upon the community by the Spirit, with prophecy among them.[25] The Greek

of the Seven Tribulations of the Order of Brothers Minor, trans. and eds. David Burr and E. Randolph Daniel (St. Bonaventure, NY: Franciscan Institute Press, 2005).

25. See 1 Cor. 11: 26 and 29. For more on this theme, see David Hill, *New Testament Prophecy* (Louisville: Westminster John Knox Press, 1979) and Wayne Grudem, *The Gift of Prophecy in the New Testament and Today* (Wheaton, IL: Crossway Books, 2000).

word used (*propheteia*) has the connotation "to speak forth" more than it signifies "foretelling."[26]

In its earliest Christian manifestation, prophecy has little to do with one's ability to predict the future. Instead, we see the earliest Christian commentators, drawing on the scriptural use of the term, describing prophecy as a particular form of expression. Prophecy is distinct from other declarative forms, not because of some unique format, but because of the grounding or source of the expression. Here we see that prophecy is intimately tied to one's ability to read, understand and interpret scripture, which is the revealed Word of God. As such, one no longer sees with the eyes of ordinary human perception, but with the spiritual senses as illumined by grace and the Word. We can see this way of understanding prophetic speech articulated in the work of Origen (d. ca. 254). While clearly Platonic in his philosophical background, Origen's understanding of prophecy is deeply rooted in one's ability to read scripture through the spiritual senses.[27] This theme is picked up and developed by others, but reaches a pinnacle of systematic articulation in the work of Augustine of Hippo (d. 430).

In Augustine's theology of prophecy, the working of grace – that is, the source of inspired intellectual vision – allows one not just to forecast future events or images, but to articulate "God-given insight into the meaning of ordinary, publicly accessible facts, whether of the present or of the past."[28] There is a sense in which Augustine is distancing

26. Niels Christian Hvidt, "Prophecy and Revelation: A Theological Survey on the Problem of Christian Prophecy," *Studia Theologica* 52 (1998): 150-151. See also, "Prophecy," in *Handbook of Biblical Criticism*, eds. Richard Soulen and R. Kendall Soulen, 3rd ed. (Louisville: Westminster John Knox Press, 2001), 142-145.

27. For example, see Origen, *De pricipiis* Bk. IV, no. 8, in *Origen: An Exhortation to Martyrdom, Prayer and Selected Works*, ed. Rowan Greer (New York: Paulist Press, 1979), 187.

28. Robert Markus, *Saeculum: History and Society in the Theology of St. Augustine* (Cambridge: Cambridge University Press, 1970), 194. Augustine further develops the Spirit's role in prophecy, that is the divine aid to intellectual vision, in *De Genesi ad Litteram* Bk. XII, 26.53; 30.58; and 31.59

his theology of prophecy from some extraordinary and limited experiences of a few to instead include all Christians as would-be prophets. Those who, aided by grace, are able to express an inspired intellectual vision of even ordinary events would see the world anew and offer a voice of truth. One need not dream or conjure images to prophesy, but rather one need only be open to the Spirit's working in one's reading of scripture, which remains the true test of authenticity of the prophet.

After Augustine there are several thinkers over the course of Christian history that appropriate and adopt the strongly Augustinian notion of prophecy as that speech that arises from seeing the world as it actually is through the reading of scripture and illumined by grace. Some of the most notable thinkers include Gregory the Great, Hugh of St. Victor and Joachim of Fiore. While a full examination of the influence of all of these thinkers and their individual contributions to the antecedent theology of prophecy inherited by Bonaventure is beyond the scope of this current project, suffice it to say that Bonaventure's sources significantly shaped the way the Seraphic Doctor constructed his Legenda Major and understood Christian prophecy.[29]

For Bonaventure the prophet is one who is able to progress in the reading of scripture to arrive at its spiritual and truest sense. In so doing, to become one who can authentically read the Book of Scripture, one becomes able to read the Book of Life and see the fuller meaning of history. This is the core of Bonaventure's understanding of prophecy. Like the earliest Christian references and subsequent patristic commentators, prophecy is not so much about foretelling as it is about seeing the world as it really is. In

29. See Bernard McGinn, *The Flowering of Mysticism: Men and Women in the New Mysticism – 1200-1350* (New York: Crossroads, 1998), 93-101. For more on the influence of these figures on Bonaventure's theology, see Daniel Horan's forthcoming article: "Bonaventure's Theology of Prophecy in the Legenda Major," *Antonianum* (2014).

other words, we might say that prophecy is about seeing the world through the "eyes of God." Bonaventure, following Augustine, holds that we are most able to do this by becoming people of scripture, imbued with God's Revelation in a way that shades and reshapes our perception. Naturally, justice becomes a primary theme that emerges in the reading of the Book of Life when, with the sense and vision of a prophet, one sees the injustice, marginalization and abuse that occurs in our world. Like the prophets of scripture, the Christian prophet "calls it as he or she sees it" or, to use yet another colloquialism, "sees it as it really is."

The prophet is himself or herself necessarily a marginal person. Although not synonymous with standing on the outskirts of society, there is a sense in which being prophetic requires the wholesale appropriation of evangelical poverty (as opposed to the abject poverty demarcated above). The more one moves from the position of privilege and wealth, of comfort and security, toward a place of solidarity with the marginalized, the more one is able to holistically embrace the call of the *vita evangelica* by following in the footsteps of Christ. It is a long process of conversion and growth that does not occur in sweeping or immediate changes. The exemplar of this way of authentic Christian living is none other than Francis of Assisi who, in Bonaventure's *Legenda Major*, becomes the prophet *par excellence*. Francis is portrayed as one like the greatest prophets of the Old Testament (Daniel, Ezekiel, Moses and Elijah) and is identified with the herald of Christ, John the Baptist. This prophetic identification occurs most strongly in chapter eleven of the *Legenda Major*, long after Francis had fully entered a place of solidarity as identified above. Francis's position in the world, one of solidarity rooted in evangelical poverty, allowed him to be more open to God's Word and therefore see the world as it really was. Bonaventure illustrates this spiritual vision in twelve narratives, each exhibiting features of prophetic confirmation in the Spirit.

What emerges from Bonaventure's portrayal of Francis the prophet as one steeped in scripture and rooted in a position of solidarity is a model for ongoing conversion and Christian living. What does it mean to be a Christian according to the example of Francis of Assisi? The answer is to live in solidarity and be a prophet. It is as a prophet, the living of the Word of God, that one is able to continually sustain a place of solidarity and speak the word of truth to a world in need of that challenge. For the contemporary Christian – our young women and men at our colleges and universities – academic community engagement as a path toward solidarity is the beginning of such a life of ongoing conversion and prophecy.

Francis's conversion to a life of solidarity with the poor, marginalized and abused exemplifies the type of lifestyle we most desire for the next generation of college graduates. A generation of young people committed to service, not out of a sense of philanthropy or condescending self-gratification, but out of identification of injustice in the world that calls for protest and committed engagement. That our students become prophets, living the Word of God in such a way that they see the world anew and speak the truth to power, is both what follows from a life of solidarity and sustains Christian living. When we offer Millennials the challenge of "profit or prophet?" we invite the next generation to transcend the limited and self-centered strictures of a profit-driven culture to enter a community of meaning rooted in the narrative of Christianity modeled in the particular life of Francis of Assisi.[30]

30. For more on the formation of a moral and ethical decision-making in light of the Christian narrative, see Stanley Hauerwas, *A Community of Character: Toward a Constructive Christian Social Ethics* (Notre Dame: University of Notre Dame Press, 1981). What I have envisioned here is a particularly Franciscan-Christian notion of ethical formation rooted in a curriculum and educational environment shaped by explicit reflection on the life and influence of Francis of Assisi and the subsequent Franciscan tradition.

Conclusion

Service in a generic sense, admirable as it may be, is but an action extrinsic to any faith commitment or exclusively Christian understanding of valued living. While one cannot expect all students to accept the challenge, live in solidarity and become people of scripture and therefore prophets, the issue for us to consider is whether or not the curriculum even provides the condition for the possibility of such conversion. The Franciscan tradition that serves as the founding charism of the AFCU institutions of higher education offers a timely and unique approach to holistic education for today's young adults. Already predisposed to service as they are, Millennials are particularly positioned to be formed in a tradition that moves beyond the concept of service toward a posture of solidarity. Encouraging community service as a component of integrated learning is not the challenge Millennials need, especially from Franciscan colleges and universities. Instead, Millennials should be challenged to move toward stepping outside the systemic structures of injustice motivated so often by profit and upward social mobility and instead position themselves in a place of solidarity. Keeping in mind that evangelical poverty is not the same as abject poverty, today's young adults should be encouraged to look at the model of Francis of Assisi and re-appropriate his way of life for contemporary living. To sustain this way of Christian living and to learn to see the world anew, Millennials should be open to the Word of God and live it in such a way as to speak the truth that comes with the call of the prophet.

Students may respond to this notion with varying degrees of enthusiasm,[31] but the condition for the possibility of some response – namely the shift in administrative dis-

---

31. See Daniel Horan, "St. Francis and the Millennials: Kindred Spirits," *St. Anthony Messenger Magazine* 118 (October 2010): 30-34.

course of service to solidarity and the challenge to be contemporary Christian prophets – should be a goal of Franciscan institutions of higher education. To integrate programs whose aim is precisely this might better enable AFCU institutions to offer a particularly Franciscan education to their students. The ongoing evaluation and (re)development of curricula and educational programs is nothing foreign to the Franciscan tradition. For Francis himself, shortly before his death, is remembered to have said, "Let us begin, brothers, to serve the Lord god, for up until now we have done little or nothing." (1C6:103).[32] Hopefully a renewed emphasis on solidarity and prophecy as constitutive elements of a Franciscan education might contribute to the shaping of the next generation of young adults into integrated members of the Christian and global community.

∾

---

32. Thomas of Celano, *The Life of Saint Francis* Bk. II, Ch. VI, v. 103, in *FAED* 1:273.

Sources for Readings

∾

Pre-Program Prayer and Reflection
Scripture: Luke 10:2-9
Franciscan: A selection from the *Life of St. Francis*, by Thomas of Celano; ch. IX, vv. 21-22 (FAED vol. I)

Day One
Scripture: Luke 9:23-25
Franciscan: A selection from *The Major Life of St. Francis*, by St. Bonaventure; ch. I, v. 4 (FAED vol. II).

Day Two
Scripture: Matthew 6:31-33
Franciscan: A selection from *The Life of St. Francis*, by Thomas of Celano; ch. XXVIII, v. 76 (FAED vol. I).

Day Three
Scripture: Matthew 6:19-21
Franciscan: A selection from *The Later Rule of 1223*, by St. Francis; ch. VI, vv. 1-4 (FAED vol. I).

Day Four
Scripture: Isaiah 58:6-8
Franciscan: A selection from *The Admonitions*, by St. Francis; ch XXVII, vv. 1-6 (FAED vol. I).

Day Five
Scripture: James 1:2-5
Franciscan: A selection from *True and Perfect Joy,* by St. Francis; vv. 1-5 (FAED vol. I).

Day Six
Scripture: 1 Peter 4:8-11
Franciscan: A selection from *The Form of Life of St. Clare of Assisi*, by St. Clare; ch. 10, vv. 6-7 (CAED).

Closing Day Prayer and Reflection
Scripture: Matthew 17:1-9
Franciscan: A selection from *The Life of St. Francis*, by Thomas of Celano; ch. XXIX v. 83 (FAED vol. I).

Post- Program Prayer and Reflection
Scripture: Matthew 9:18-25
Franciscan: A selection from *The Testament*, by St. Francis; vv. 1-3, 20-21, 40-41 (FAED vol. I).

∾

Notes & Reflections

Notes & Reflections

Notes & Reflections

Notes & Reflections

Notes & Reflections

Notes & Reflections

Notes & Reflections

Notes & Reflections

Notes & Reflections

Notes & Reflections

Notes & Reflections

Notes & Reflections

Notes & Reflections

Notes & Reflections

Notes & Reflections

Notes & Reflections

Notes & Reflections

Notes & Reflections

Notes & Reflections

Notes & Reflections

Notes & Reflections

Notes & Reflections

Notes & Reflections

Notes & Reflections

Notes & Reflections

Notes & Reflections

Notes & Reflections

Notes & Reflections

Notes & Reflections

About the Authors

∾

Daniel P. Horan, OFM is a Franciscan friar of Holy Name Province , a columinst for *America* magazine, and the author of several books including: *The Last Words of Jesus: A Meditation of Love and Suffering* (2013), *Francis of Assisi and the Future of Faith: Exploring Franciscan Spirituality and Theology in the Modern World* (2012), and *Dating God: Live and Love in the Way of St. Francis* (2012). He is currently working on a Ph.D. in Systematic Theology at Boston College and earned an M.A. and M.Div. degrees from the Washington Theological Union and an Honors B.A. in Theology from St. Bonaventure University. To learn more about his academic and popular work, visit www.DanHoran.com.

Julianne E. Wallace is the associate director of Faith Formation, Worship, and Ministry at St. Bonaventure University, a Franciscan University in Western New York Sate. She earned an M.T.S. from the Washington Theological Union and a B.A. in Music from Mary Washington College in Virginia. She has led many service trips and served as a Franciscan Volunteer Minister in Wilmington, DE.

Advance Praise for *Spirit and Life*

∾

"*Spirit and Life* is great gift to all those who facilitate immersion experiences. Those new to the work will benefit from the theologically sound, sequential, tested, and thoroughly adaptable structure; experienced practitioners will be blessed by the rich collection of prayers, Scripture readings, reflection questions, and thoughtfully selected texts from the Franciscan tradition. *Spirit and Life* is an extraordinary resource. It will serve as a significant contribution to this important work for years to come."
— MICHAEL LOVETTE-COLYER, Ph.D., Assistant Vice President and Director of University Ministry, University of San Diego

"*Spirit and Life* is an invaluable resource for any minister leading service experiences. It masterfully uses scripture to help participants connect the life of Christ to their experiences and threads Franciscan spirituality throughout in a gentle, inviting and utterly compelling way."
— SUSAN HAARMAN, Faith and Justice Campus Minister, Loyola University Chicago

"This resource is a rich, compelling, and eminently usable guide for any 'pilgrim' on an immersion-style experience. The authors offer the Franciscan tradition as a powerful framework for an encounter with poverty, an experience of service, or simply a journey in community. I have no doubt that many students (and teachers alike!) will benefit from the rituals, reflections, and challenging questions found in this guide to the spirituality of solidarity."
— DAVID GOLEMBOSKI, Chair of the Board, Witness for Peace; and 2007 Recipient of USCCB Cardinal Bernardin New Leadership Award

"Dan and Julianne provide us with a unique creation: a process for people in any experience, meeting each person where he or she is, fostering prayerful reflection, inviting growth, and leading to solidarity. This resource encourages making immersion experiences more than a onetime encounter. Here, the value of integrating immersion experiences into our lives is celebrated and demonstrated to bolster relationships with God and with those once considered 'Other' now known to be Sister and Brother."
— KATIE SULLIVAN, Executive Director, Franciscan Volunteer Ministry

"Horan and Wallace provide a simple, but inclusive method for spiritual reflection in the Franciscan tradition. The text, intended for college-age students who have participated in or will participate in a period of immersion in impoverished areas, provides a very usable format to internalize the lived experience. Each reflection includes quiet and community prayer, both a scripture reading and a reading from the Franciscan sources as well as time and space for written reflection and group sharing."
— SR. MARGARET KLOTZ, O.S.F., Director of the Franciscan Center, Cardinal Stritch University

"*Spirit and Life* is something that every campus minister should not only have on their shelves but use for every service experience they plan. As someone who created a reflection guide for a weekend service trip I know how important it is to have theological reflection as a part of every service experience no matter what the age of the participants. Now I don't have to reinvent the wheel. I will gladly and enthusiastically use this guide and buy it for all my college students. *Spirit and Life* will be a resource and time capsule of each experience that I take with my college students. And for young adults, it will be something they will return to again and again. It will remind them of the experience they had and also of how they felt and where God was in the midst of it all. St. Francis is so accessible to people so even those that do not have a background in Franciscan Studies as I do will appreciate and come to know more about this popular saint. A true gem."
— COURTNEY HULL, Campus Minister, Mansfield University

Made in the USA
Middletown, DE
10 March 2015